The Bear Essentials

ISBN: 1-58173-496-4

Design by Pat Covert and Miles G. Parsons

Printed in The United States of America

THE BEAR
ESSENTIALS

THE BEAR ESSENTIALS

THE CAREER AND CHARACTER OF PAUL "BEAR" BRYANT

Vick Cross

CONTENTS

*"I ain't never been nothing
but a winner."*

PAUL "BEAR" BRYANT

THE ESSENTIAL BEAR

Paul "Bear" Bryant was driven by an intense determination, a passion to control and dominate. "I have never, never seen a man so opposed to losing," said Steve Sloan, who played for him and coached against him.

Bryant was an immensely deep and complex man. He has been written about and analyzed obsessively, but no one has yet explained the deep ironies and contrasts in his personality.

What drove him? He told John Underwood he never forgot the town boys who laughed at him and his mother when they brought their mule cart full of vegetables into Fordyce, Arkansas, to sell. "I still remember the ones that did it," he said. He hated the poverty from which he came and, contrary to all reason, was never confident that he would not somehow return to it.

And yet he seemed self-confident to the point of

arrogance. One of his players told me, "I don't think that
he thought that he could do anything wrong ... but to
him it did not really matter. 'If I did it wrong, it's okay,
I'm Paul Bryant. It'll be all right, y'all will just have to ...
ignore it. I'm not going to worry about it.'"

Coach Bryant had an unmatched ability to pierce
the hearts of young men and make them believe. He
talked endlessly, some would say ad nauseum, to his
players about the things that mattered to him: showing
class, going to church, honoring parents. But he was
prone to profanity and sometimes drank himself to
oblivion, hardly a class act. He loved to shoot dice, play
golf for money, and bet on horses. There were rumors
about women.

Clearly, he felt pressure, mostly self-inflicted. He
would sometimes say to his players that he would fire
them before he ever got fired himself. He demanded
effort, complete effort at all times: 100 percent during
every repetition of every drill in every practice; 100
percent on every play of every game.

He didn't understand and could not abide loafing.
"Only five or six plays decide the outcome of a game," he
would tell his players. "You can't know which ones they
will be. How can you be sure you will do your best on
those plays if you don't do your best on every play?"

Bryant was big enough to take public responsibility

for errors and losses, and he often did so. But there is the slight suspicion that deep down he felt that if everyone had given as much effort as he would have himself, there would have been no errors and no losses.

He could be warm and engaging and then inexplicably cruel and biting to the same person within hours. He might greet a player in the hall or the dorm and ask how he was doing, or walk by the same player without even a nod. In his younger days, he took joy in driving a slacking linebacker into the ground with his unpadded shoulder. But he was not averse to the occasional hug to a visitor.

He remembered his players and even his scrubs and managers as if they were family. Many were astonished to be greeted and called by name years after their time with Bryant. A player who was having a tough time might get a call, a card, or a loan. Nothing was too much.

What Coach Bryant did for his adopted state and university was to demonstrate that, even in the South, it was possible to excel. Yes, what he led them to excel at was just a game. But the lessons he imparted extend far beyond football.

The essential Bear Bryant was a man for all time.

> *"All I had was football. I hung on as though it were life or death, which it was."*
>
> Paul Bryant

His Favorite Things

A newspaper in St. Petersburg, Florida, asked coaches around the nation to list their favorite things. Here is how Coach Bryant responded:

Favorite Food: Steak
Favorite Books: Mysteries
Favorite Movies: Musical comedies
Favorite Music: Dixieland
Favorite Leisure Activity: Golf

The Porkpie Hat

Coach Bryant wore an old brown fedora and baseball hats in his early career. Sonny Werblin, owner of the New York Jets, gave Bryant his first houndstooth porkpie hat at around the time Werblin shocked the NFL by signing Joe Namath for $427,000.

Bryant loved the hat, and Werblin later sent him several more in different colors.

CRYING LIKE BABIES

Ellis Beck, a halfback from Ozark who played in the seventies, later worked for the alumni affairs office and accompanied Coach Bryant on speaking visits in the off-season.

Invariably, the former players who introduced Bryant, Beck says, would become tearful, and so would the audience. Why?

"If you knew him, you would not need an explanation," Beck wrote.

> *"When you are with him, you feel like you are walking with history."*
> *Boyd McWhorter*

"WE'VE GOT YOU NOW."

Bryant worked his teams so hard and long that they soon became better conditioned than opponents with less ambitious physical programs. Rather than have fun at practice, he told them, let's have fun by winning.

Toward the fourth quarter, opponents would begin to flag. Then, Gary O'Steen remembered, "You'd just sit there and laugh at them ... these old boys sucking wind, we'd say, 'Oh boy, we've got you now.' That was one of the best feelings in the world."

> *"His practices were so highly organized. He had the field divided off into eight areas, and a schedule he put up with six 20-minute periods. It was precision. When they blew that whistle, I don't care if you had 100 yards to get to the next field, you had about one minute to get there and if you didn't, someone was camping on your hiney."*
>
> *Don Heath*

TEAM RULES

Jim Blevins, a veteran of the Korean War, had this exchange with Bryant:

Bryant: "I understand you were in Korea. Did you pick up any bad habits when you were in the Army?"

Blevins: "I beg your pardon?"

Bryant: "Did you pick up any bad habits in the Army?"

Blevins: "What would be a bad habit?"

Bryant: "Smoking."

Blevins: "Nossir, I don't smoke."

Bryant: "Do you drink?"

Blevins: "Yessir, I'll drink a beer now and then."

Bryant: "Well, if you feel like you need one, come out to the house, because that way you won't get into any trouble. So you won't embarrass the team or anything."

"I have tried to teach them to show class, to have pride, and to display character. I think football, winning games, takes care of itself if you do that."
                                    Paul Bryant

THE MOTIVATOR

HANDS ON

Bryant's Kentucky Wildcats were leading a superior Florida team at Gainesville, but the heat was prostrating. Bryant told Assistant Coach Ermal Allen that the team needed pumping up. Allen says he suggested Bryant start with Gene Donaldson, a 235-pound guard who was slumped almost prostrate on the dressing room floor.

Bryant bent over, picked Donaldson up in his arms, and growled: "Well, son, you gonna suck it up out there in the second half, or ain't you?"

The Wildcats held on to win.

> "[Coach Bryant] said, 'There's pain in this game,
> but the ones who win are the ones who can play
> with pain.' So he taught us to play with pain."
> Jerre Brannen

IRON LUNG

In 1958, Bryant visited Gary Banister, a ten-year-old boy, in his hospital room. Banister was confined to an iron lung, totally paralyzed.

All Bryant said was: "If you ever want to make anything out of yourself, you are going to have to get out of that contraption first."

Banister got out of the contraption. He earned a football scholarship at Alabama, though he never played football for Bryant. But except for his father and Jesus Christ, Banister wrote, no one had a greater influence on him than the Bear.

> *"Some day, life will get tough for you. You'll be two months late on your house payment, your car will quit, you won't have a job, your wife tells you she loves someone else. That's when you'll find out what you're made of. What are you going to do then? Quit? That's when you'll learn what I'm trying to do."*
>
> *Paul Bryant*

THE MUSTARD SEED

Before a big game against SMU, the eighth game in his first year at Texas A&M, Bryant visited the athletic dorm in the middle of the night and rousted his players from their beds.

Bryant surprised them by opening a Bible and quoting from St. Matthew, Chapter 17:

"'It was because you do not have enough faith,' answered Jesus. 'Remember this! If you have faith as big as a mustard seed, you will be able to say to a hill, "Go from here to there!" and it will go. You can do anything!'"

He then passed out to each of the players a tiny capsule containing a mustard seed, asked them to save them, and to look at them when they felt the urge. Then he said good night and left.

Gene Stallings remembered, "There we were, in our pajamas and skivvies, rooted in the lobby of our dorm, all wide-eyed and almost afraid to look at each other ... It was a long night for most of us because we were too excited to sleep, and God knows how many of us picked up his mustard seed capsule and studied it."

The Aggies, underdogs by four touchdowns, lost to SMU 6-3. But none of them ever forgot the mustard seed.

*"We were scared to death of him, but not in the
way that sounds. What we were really afraid of
was not pleasing him, not living up to his
expectations for us."*

Tom Somerville

Cocktails in the Potted Plants

Bryant had a huge suite in a hotel in Washington,
D.C., where admirers had staged a testimonial dinner in
1982. After the dinner, many of the players were invited
to the suite to greet the Bear and tell lies about the past.

For the entire length of the hallway leading to the
Bear's suite, writer Mickey Herskowitz observed cocktail
glasses abandoned among the potted plants and decorator
tables. Bryant's former players—some of them out of
college for twenty-five years or more—couldn't bring
themselves to greet their old mentor with alcoholic drinks
in their hands.

*"My biggest thrill in college was when he called
me by name on the field."*

Keith Pugh

NOT LIKE EVERYONE ELSE

In the seventies, when longer hair on men came into fashion, Bryant asked some of his players why they wanted to let their hair grow out.

"To be like everyone else," they said.

"If you were like everyone else," Bear growled, "I wouldn't have you here."

> *"Football teaches a boy to win, to work for maybe the first time in his life and sacrifice and suck up his guts when he's behind. It's the only place left where you can learn that."*
>
> Paul Bryant

SHOWMAN

Upon his arrival at Texas A&M, Coach Bryant displayed a talent for showmanship that he cultivated and used when he needed it.

Seldom did he use it so extravagantly as on his arrival at College Station.

A crowd of more than three thousand had gathered to meet his plane, and when it finally arrived, the fans escorted him to his hotel, where he signed in as "Paul W.

Bryant, Head Coach, Texas A&M University, College Station, Texas."

By the time he arrived at the Sacred Grove outdoor theater, the assembled crowd had grown to five thousand, ready to scream for the new coach.

Bryant gave them what they wanted. He tore off his coat, and stomped on it. He ripped off his tie, and stomped on it, too. The Aggies were going wild before he said a word.

EVOLUTION

Bryant's long time trainer at Alabama, Jim Goostree, saw the coach's style evolve through the years. On one occasion during Alabama's slide to two straight 6-5 seasons in the 1970s, Goostree got thirty minutes on Bryant's schedule for a consultant to present a motivational program being used in the industry.

Bryant, Goostree said, was fascinated by what the consultants told him and the meeting stretched into the late afternoon. Presented with some data on motivational rewards, Bryant would say, "I never knew what I was doing, but I'm the best at that."

From that time on, Goostree said, Bryant seemed to him to emphasize positive motivation as opposed to the purely physical style he had used as a younger man.

"The first thing that he would talk about with his squad each fall, in his team meeting, was to have a plan for everything. And then he would start talking about the spiritual part of it, the physical part of it, and writing your mother. About having a plan, a plan for practice, a plan for the classroom. And just through pure repetition [he built] belief in the plan."

In later years, Bryant was more likely to leave the details of coaching to his assistants and concentrate on motivation.

> *"[Coach Bryant] had something in his mind, he knew what his reaction was going to be if we were ahead, or we were behind, or playing poorly or playing well ... he had already thought out ... he had a tremendous ability to recognize the emotional aspect of the players and of the team, and he knew and thought about what that emotional aspect was as he went into that game, and he knew he had something in his mind that he was going to do ... whatever the circumstances presented."*
>
> *Bobby D. Keith*

JUST A FEW WORDS

Bryant's stature and reputation were such that only a few words were needed to motivate a player.

He did it with Jeremiah Castille when Castille was just a freshman.

"I believe in you. I believe you can play," Bryant told him.

For Castille, who grew up in a dysfunctional family in Phenix City, having Bryant express confidence in him was a spur to earn All-America honors and a place on the Tide's Team of the Century.

THE TOUGH GUY

THE REAL BEAR

It was a scrawny, tired bear. But it was a real bear. To fourteen-year-old Paul Bryant, it looked thirty feet tall.

But the promoter at the Lyric Theater in Fordyce, Arkansas, was offering one dollar a minute for anyone who would get on stage and wrestle the bear. To Paul, who was making fifty cents a day chopping cotton, that sounded like a fortune. He said he would do it.

He was a tough, rawboned, clumsy, and entirely unsophisticated country boy. A mama's boy, he called himself, because his father was often ill, and his mother had to be the disciplinarian.

No doubt Mama would have vetoed the idea of Paul wrestling a bear. But she wasn't there, and some pretty local girls were. And Paul always did what he said he would do.

Taking the stage, he charged the bear, knocked it flat, and hung on for dear life.

Time was passing. The bear got loose, and Paul knocked it down again. Then the bear's muzzle came off. In the clinch, it began to chew on Paul's ear.

Paul jumped into the front row seats, badly barking his shins, and took off.

By the time things settled down, the bear and the promoter were gone. Paul never got paid, but he got a nickname for life.

> *On why he was so competitive:*
> *"Hell, I don't know. All I know is, if you have on a different color jersey than me, I want to beat your ass."*
>
> *Paul Bryant*

THE FIRST LICK

When he was still in high school, the young Bear got a job working at a factory that made spokes for automobile wheels in Parma, Arkansas, his aunt's hometown.

He evidently made an enemy of what he said was a "large blond boy" who accused him of "dating his girl."

Once, after picking up his paycheck, Bryant was confronted by his rival outside the factory.

Bear, as he always would, had a plan. Get in the first lick. When the boy started to say something, Bryant said, "I put my fist in his mouth." That ended the fight.

> *"He can take his'n and beat your'n—or he can take your'n and beat his'n."*
>
> Jake Gaither

SIX MILES TO KINGSLAND

It was six miles from Fordyce to Kingsland. Bryant and some other boys were arguing about how long it would take to run there. Bear bet the bunch he could make it there in less than thirty minutes.

In 100° heat, Bryant took off. He made it, and collapsed, in just over twenty-nine minutes.

> *"When Coach Bryant goes to war, he doesn't just bring the rifles. He brings the howitzers."*
>
> Howard Schnellenberger

THE DRESSING ROOM DOOR

Jim Bowman was a freshman manager for the 1965 Alabama team.

Playing Tennessee in Birmingham, the Tide was inside the ten-yard-line when Ken Stabler lost count of the downs and tried to stop the clock by throwing away a pass. The ball went over to the Vols, and the game ended in a 7-7 tie.

Bryant was furiously disappointed.

Bowman had forgotten that he had the only key to the dressing room. He ran off to get the game ball back from the Tennessee managers.

When he finally got back to the dressing room, the door had been broken down and wrenched off its hinges. By Coach Bryant.

Inside, Bryant apologized to his players for the confusion on the sidelines.

> *"He literally knocked the door down. I mean right off its hinges. A policeman came in and asked who knocked the door down, and Coach Bryant said, 'I did.' The policeman just said, 'Okay,' and walked off."*
>
> *Jerry Duncan*

THE JUNCTION PATTERN

The notorious "gut-check" at the little town of Junction, Texas, is one of the best known chapters in Bear Bryant's life. Whole books have been written about those ten days of hell in 1954.

Bryant took two busloads of players to the dusty, rocky little town 330 miles from the Texas A&M campus. Only one busload, twenty-nine players, returned.

At one point, every one of the team's centers quit, including Fred Broussard, who was considered a pro prospect.

"Goodbye, goodbye, bless your hearts, goodbye," the Bear told them, shaking each one by the hand. He turned Lloyd Hale, a sophomore guard, into an all-conference center.

But Bryant's players at Kentucky and Alabama can tell you that Junction was not in itself unique. Bryant's approach to football, wherever he was, was consistent. Give 100 percent, or else. "My plan was to bleed 'em and gut 'em because I didn't want any well-wishers hanging around," he said about his first Alabama team.

At Kentucky in 1946, Bryant put his players through long, vicious practices and weeded a team out of perhaps two hundred who tried out. Bryant himself worked like a demon, sleeping no more than four hours a night and driving his assistant coaches unmercifully. One staff meeting lasted until 4:00 a.m.

Only thirty-two years old then, the Bear gloried in taking on a young player himself, pads or no pads. Some players hated him, and not all quite forgave him for his relentless intensity. "He worked us like we were getting ready to fight the Japanese all over again," said Walt Jaworski, a freshman in 1947.

It was no different at Alabama in 1958. In the spring, Bryant gave tryouts to as many as a hundred, and he was brutally frank with the seniors on the team, telling them they'd have to be twice as good as the younger players to earn a roster spot because his eye was on the future.

Dozens of players quit or were excused, and many of them were among the best real athletes on the team. Bryant said at one point the "riffraff" were weeding themselves out. To the Bear, an athlete who didn't play at full speed at all times was "riffraff."

> *"If a man is a quitter, I'd rather find out in practice than in a game. I ask for all a player has, so I'll know later what I can expect."*
> *Paul Bryant*

The Tough Guy

A COMMANDING PRESENCE

The first time George Blanda saw the Bear, he thought, "This must be what God looks like."

The Bear was a big man, and he had a commanding presence. Most people were afraid of him. His coaches and players found him intimidating and would avoid direct contact when they could.

Almost no one called him Bear to his face. One would preface a question with "Coach," and respond to a question with "Yes, sir."

On a podium or in front of reporters, his voice was often an inaudible bass. If asked what he believed to be a stupid question, he was biting.

A reporter once asked him if he would require his players to carry a football around campus at all times to prevent fumbling.

"Well, that certainly is a stupid question," he said. "Let's see if I can think of a suitably stupid answer."

There were no more questions that day.

> *"There was no way I was about to hire Bear. In no time, he'd have slit my throat, drank my blood, and had my job."*
>
> Frank Howard

A DISDAIN FOR QUITTERS

In 1958, his first year at Alabama, Bryant ran a rigorous and unrelenting campaign of conditioning, and before the players arrived for fall practice, he instructed almost everyone to report at a specified weight.

The weight specified was, in most cases, much lower than the players had carried when playing for the former Alabama coach J.B. "Ears" Whitworth. Quite a few players struggled to meet the requirement, and inevitably some failed.

Given a second chance, several still remained too heavy. These were men who had been regarded among the most talented athletes on the team. Bryant kicked them out of the dorm and off the team.

A few days later, Bert Bank, Bryant's radio producer, met the coach for breakfast at 5:30 a.m. at the Stafford Hotel in Tuscaloosa.

One of the dismissed players was working at the Stafford as a bellman, and he greeted the men cordially as they crossed the lobby. Bank said hello, but Bryant cut the young man dead.

Bank asked Bryant if he wasn't being a little harsh.

"He's a quitter," the coach said. "Hell, I wouldn't let him carry my suitcase in here. If I was supposed to be on the fifth floor, he'd be liable to leave it on the second."

"Bryant says his [kind of football] is 'an eye for an eye.' Bear must be softening up a bit because I heard his Texas A&M squad never offered an eye unless they could get two in exchange."

Harry Mehre

THE BROKEN LEG

In 1935, while playing at the University of Alabama, Bryant broke a small bone in his leg (the fibula) in a game against Mississippi State.

No one thought he would play the next week against bitter rival Tennessee. Though he had no idea of playing himself, Bryant went to the game and put on his uniform.

In those days, most players wore a different number every game. Bryant said later it was so they could sell more programs.

Coach Hank Crisp, invited to make a short talk before the game, said: "I'll tell you gentlemen one thing. I don't know what you're going to do. But I know one damn thing. Old 34 will be after 'em. He'll be after their asses."

Bryant looked down at his jersey. He was number 34! After the build-up, he had no choice. He played the entire game, caught some passes, and made some key blocks.

Ralph McGill, an Atlanta newspaper writer at the

time, went so far as to ask to see the X-rays to verify the injury. He was convinced.

The feat made Bryant famous, and he played the rest of the year with the broken bone.

"I was lucky as a priest," he said.

> *"He made me aware that when you're caught up in the heat of a game, you realize just who you can depend on, who's willing to pay the price."*
> Paul Crane

ENIGMA

Charlie McClendon says he felt very close to Coach Bryant after a long conversation that took place when McClendon was driving him home from a speaking engagement. Tears were shed, McClendon said.

The next day, Coach Bryant cut McClendon dead in the hallway at the athletic department. Didn't acknowledge him at all when he said hello.

McClendon decided that Bryant just didn't want him to feel too close.

"Paul Bryant was a man of many moods ... he could turn them off and on in a matter of seconds. He was a Jekyll and Hyde."

Jim Goostree

NONE OF YOUR DAMN BUSINESS

Bryant's good friend and long-time radio producer Bert Bank was at practice in 1958 when a fight broke out between two linemen, Jim Blevins and Johnny (Red) Gann. Blevins hit Gann in the mouth and knocked out four teeth. Gann's parents were in the stands, also watching practice.

Later, Bank asked Bryant why he didn't stop the fight. "None of your damn business," Bryant told him.

Responding to a coach about a recruit who was having it tough deciding where to go to college: "He'd better be tough if he's going to come down and put on the red shirt."

Paul Bryant

BROKEN NOSE: NO PROBLEM

Gary Phillips, who played for Bryant's first team at Alabama, had suffered a broken nose in practice. "It swelled really wide and was sore and blue," he remembered.

Coming down the steps toward practice, Bryant said, "Well, little buddy, how's your nose?"

Phillips, hopeful he'd be given a break in practice, told Bryant, "It's pretty sore, coach."

"Well, you're just handicapped," Bryant said. Phillips practiced in pads.

> *"Playing for Bear was like going to war. You may come out of it intact, but you'll never forget the experience."*
>
> *George Blanda*

NO CONTROL

A disappointed Alabama fan once wrote Bryant complaining that the Tide cheerleaders were yelling, "Go to Hell, Ole Miss."

Bryant responded, saying he was so busy he didn't hear cheers, and that in any event, "I am charged with responsibility for the actions of the players and have no control over the other students."

> *After Kentucky lost to Santa Clara in the Orange Bowl in 1950:*
> *"I'm a win man myself. I don't go for place or show."*
>
> Paul Bryant

EAT NAILS

Christ Vagotis, who played at Alabama on two national championship teams in the sixties, took a four-day weekend to New Orleans just before spring practice. He had told everyone that he was going home.

When he got back, he had a note from Coach Bryant, who threw him out of the dorm and cut off his dining privileges.

Christ saw Bryant again and asked what sort of diet he should follow, since he wasn't eating training table food.

"If you want to play for Alabama, eat nails and sleep in the woods," Bryant told him.

TWO ORANGE BOWL LOSSES

Many coaches use bowl invitations as an excuse to practice for an additional three weeks, thus gaining an edge for the next season. After a tough year of practice, players generally deplore that idea, preferring to think of a bowl game as a reward.

Some of Bryant's former players say he overworked his team before two Orange Bowl games.

In the first, Bryant's Kentucky team fell to Santa Clara after he restricted his players from recreational visits to the beach and made them practice hard in pads. Santa Clara won, 21-13. Bryant himself, in *Bear*, said he had been "pigheaded."

Then before the 1972 Orange Bowl, Bryant again kept his players away from the beaches and the bright lights of Miami under the apparent theory that having been caged up, they would come out of the dressing room like lions. Meanwhile, the Nebraska team was reported to be at the Playboy Club, on the beach, and at the Jai Alai fronton.

It backfired. "Our rear ends were so tight we couldn't even walk," John Croyle later told John Bolton. "We went to movies. We said, 'Crap, we can go to movies in Tuscaloosa.'"

Nebraska probably had a better team, but the 38-6 whipping was worse than it should have been.

A MAN ALOOF

George Washington was said to have stood apart and above all of his contemporaries, and Bryant was the same.

Assistant Coach Robert Ford once made the mistake of asking the coach, in a jocular manner, "Hey Coach, what's the hurry?"

The whole dressing room grew quiet. "What did you say?" Bryant barked.

In too deep, Ford could only repeat the question. Bryant slammed his locker shut and never replied.

THE SOFTIE

THE DEAD DOG

The story of the little boys and their dog was told in several versions. Elmer Smith told it this way in a book written by Mike Bynum and Jerry Brondfield. It happened near College Station, Texas.

Bryant always arrived early at the office, and sometimes he would ask the first assistant coach to arrive to take a ride with him and eat some breakfast.

One morning, the Coach (still driving himself in those days) took a road that was unfamiliar to Smith. He stopped in front of a shack where two small boys were sitting on the stoop.

Smith said Bryant got out of the car, walked over to the boys, put his arms around them, and talked to them a while.

When he got back to the car, Smith asked him what it was all about.

Coach Bryant said he had run over a dog on the same road earlier that morning, and since there was only one house anywhere around, he decided the dog must have belonged to those little boys.

"So I came back here, and ... I promised those kids they'd have another dog before the next night."

Smith said Bryant did little work that day. He was too busy finding a dog.

> *"No one will ever know how many trips he made*
> *to Children's Hospital in Birmingham or how*
> *many letters he wrote and long-distance*
> *telephone calls he made to sick children."*
>
> Billy Varner

MARY HARMON BRYANT

The young Bear was a ladies' man and loved telling the story of a trip he and some other players took on a riverboat with a group of Chi Omegas in 1935.

It took the "prettiest girl on campus," Mary Harmon Black, to settle him down.

When Bryant first asked Mary Harmon for a date, she consulted her calendar and suggested something several weeks away.

Bryant "got his back up" and walked away. He had meant now, tonight.

A little later, he got a call at the dorm. Mary Harmon was available that evening.

> *"The first thing a coach needs starting out is a wife who is willing to put up with a lot of neglect."*
>
> Paul Bryant

BRYANT SCHOLARSHIPS

The Bear, with a $1 million gift, established a scholarship fund at Alabama that permits the children of former Alabama players to attend the University without paying tuition. More than seven hundred have taken advantage of the privilege. In 2005 there were around ninety students enrolled under the program.

> *"If I had my choice of either winning the game or winning the faith of a young man, I would choose the latter. There is no greater reward for a coach than to see his players achieve their goals in life and to know he had some small part in the success of the young men's endeavors."*
>
> Paul Bryant

BE SWEET, ANGEL

A man obsessed with his job, Bryant was never what one would call a family man. He worked incessantly, in season and off-season. And except for trips to his lakehouse on occasion with Mary Harmon, he was not much for family get-togethers.

But he was a loving father in his own way. His son, Paul Jr., was sickly as a child, and no athlete. Some athletic fathers might have pushed a son toward sports. But Bryant let Paul Jr. find his way to his considerable success in business.

When he was in the Navy in the early forties, Bryant wrote his daughter, Mae Martin, the following: "I certainly would have liked to see your Easter outfit. I know it was precious. Thanks for your letter. You were sweet to write. I miss you and MH more and more. Be sweet, angel."

When his son, Paul Jr., was a young boy, Bryant often would pose friendly questions in his postcards: "What is the Buckeye State? What is the Peach State?"

"Son, what is the hat state? Also the shoe state? I know the answer, and I'm sure you do."

Bryant signed his postcards to his children "Daddie" or "Pop."

The Softie

*"I'm just a simple plow hand from Arkansas, but
I have learned over the years how to hold a team
together. How to lift some men up, how to calm
others down, until finally they've got one
heartbeat."*

Paul Bryant

WHAT'S IMPORTANT

Thomas Prestwood Jr., a transfer from Florida State,
was determined to play for Alabama, even after four knee
operations.

Bryant wouldn't allow him to play.

"I don't want you to ruin your leg," he said.

Angry then, Prestwood later understood that Bryant
was looking out for his best interests.

*"Have a plan for everything. Expect the
unexpected. What are you going to do if your
man breaks your nose on the first play, and what
will you do if you break his arm on the first play?
Have a plan for anything that happens."*

Paul Bryant

THE BAILEY CHARTER

When Coach Sam Bailey's wife, Mildred, learned that her mother was ill in Arkansas, she began to drive west to be with her. Coach Bryant called, had her stopped in Columbus, Mississippi, and sent a chartered plane to take her the rest of the way.

Mrs. Bailey's mother died in surgery the next day.

OLD SCHOOL ON MONEY

In these days of multi-million dollar contracts for college football coaches, it's almost quaint to remember Bryant's determination to never accept a salary that was more than that paid to the president of the University.

EASY COME, EASY GO

Bryant would sometimes call his radio producer, Bert Bank, and ask him, "Bert, when was the last time I got a check? What do you owe me?"

"I'd say, '$400 or [whatever],'" Bank recalled, "and he'd say, 'Send X dollars to [a former player]; he's having trouble, and send a check to my sister in Arkansas.'"

DON'T WANT YOU BLAMING ME

Halfback Richard Strum had badly banged up his knee, but still wanted to play. Bryant called him to his office, but did not ask him to sit down.

"I've talked to Dr. Sherrill about you," he told Strum. "I was told by Dr. Sherrill that if you were to get a hard lick on your knee, that you would probably walk with a limp for the rest of your life."

Strum said, "Well, coach, I think it's going to get better."

"No, I don't want you, in your later years, if you get your leg hurt, and every morning you get up [and] put on your pants, you cuss this school and me."

"He said, 'Just remember this. I want you to finish school,'" Strum said. "'As long you remember you are part of the team and don't do anything to reflect badly on the athletic department, you'll keep getting my scholarship.'"

But Strum was surprised when he found out that he and another injured player were expected to help bus tables in the athletic department dining room to retain their scholarships.

THE FUNNY MAN

11 INCHES TALL

Halfback Duff Morrison, playing before there was platoon football, expressed to Bryant some concern that he would be unable to block a much taller Penn State player in the Liberty Bowl.

"Duff, he's only 11 inches tall when he's flat on his back," Bryant told him, "and that's where I want you to put him."

NOT AFRAID

Coach Bryant was always gracious to people who had worked for him. When I was a cub sportswriter, he granted me a telephone interview regarding an upcoming game with Georgia.

I asked him what he was most afraid of in the Bulldogs.

"Heck, I'm not afraid," he said, "I don't have to play."

No, You Couldn't

Bryant always hired great coaching staffs. Once Bert Bank told him he thought he could probably win games with assistants like Elmer Smith, Jerry Claiborne, Bebes Stallings, and Phil Cutchin.

The Bear gave him a look. "No, you couldn't," he said.

One-upmanship

The 1968 Cotton Bowl saw Bryant's Alabama team pitted again Texas A&M. The Aggies, who topped the Tide 20-16, were led by Bryant's former star assistant, Gene Stallings. Following the game, the two coaches faced a joint press conference.

Stallings got to the conference a little late, still dressed in his coaching gear, while Bryant was dressed up. The press obviously noticed the contrast, and everything came to a standstill as Bryant said, "I refuse to have my picture taken with anybody who looks like that!"

Stallings came on in and sat down, but the attention was obviously focused on Bryant, who would periodically say, "Somebody ask Bebes something, will ya?" The press would ask Stallings a token question, and return to Bryant, who would eventually say again, "Ask Bebes something."

Another press conference was scheduled for the next day, and this time Stallings decided "I'm going to upstage Coach Bryant if it's the last thing I do—I'm going to that press conference in a tux!"

Stallings carried a tuxedo to practice and put it on afterwards, then left for the press conference. When he entered, thinking he had bested Bryant, he was surprised to find Bryant wearing a cowboy hat, an open shirt with a scarf around his neck, and boots. And the boots had Texas Aggies on them.

Stallings reported that, "Not one soul noticed that I had a tux on when I walked in!"

WRAPUP

In late December of 1971, Bryant was a guest of long-time friend Curt Gowdy at Sedgewick Farms in Selma, Alabama, for a taping of Gowdy's *American Sportsman* program.

Plans were interrupted because of the heavy rain that had soaked the area, and Bryant could not stay longer because Alabama was scheduled to play Nebraska in the Orange Bowl on New Year's Day. But he promised to return to finish the hunt.

On January 2, 1972, Bryant returned to Sedgewick Farms, despite Alabama's disappointing 38-6 loss to Nebraska. He and Gowdy were hunting with a champion pointer named Wrapup, who disappeared in the tall grass. When they found him two hours later, he was still on point. Appreciating the dog's effort, Bryant wryly suggested that perhaps he might recruit Wrapup as a cornerback.

REMEMBERING HIS ROOTS

An Inferiority Complex

Young Paul Bryant worked hard on his family's farm, plowing before and after school each day. On Saturday, he hitched up the wagon and mule and went to Fordyce with his mama. He didn't mind the work, but admitted that "What I hated about it was coming face-to-face with the people we met along the way. I had an inferiority complex. I didn't feel like I was as good as those people. I thought they looked down on me."

> *"I have said it many a time, I do love the football. I really do. Lord knows where I'd be without it. Probably back in Arkansas pushing a plow."*
> *Paul Bryant*

HOLES IN HIS SHIRTS

In the days following the 1979 Sugar Bowl and the famous goal line stand, there was a victory party in the coach's suite at the Hyatt. Bryant wore what was obviously a new T-shirt, yet it had a hole in it. One of the guests called his attention to it, saying, "Coach, your shirt has a hole in it." He replied by saying, "Yes, I know. I always tear a small hole in my T-shirts, so I'll never forget where I came from."

> *"He had an uncommon goodness about him, and he never forgot his roots."*
>
> *Aruns Callery*

X'S AND O'S

TECHNIQUES

Bryant was never thought of as a genius of strategic football. What he could do was recognize a successful innovation and adapt it to his own circumstances: use of the wishbone, for example, or gradually moving to larger linemen when the passing game became more important.

Motivation was, of course, his strongest point. Many stories—a lot of them retold in this history—testify to his ability to read his players and take just the right action at the right time.

But there was another area in which he excelled, one many football fans are not aware of. That was his mastery of what is known as football "techniques."

Bryant's innovation—one he may have borrowed from Bum Phillips—was to number and describe the various hand, foot, and arm movements players would use in a given situation.

The book *Bear Bryant on Winning Football* (written cover to cover by Gene Stallings, though Bryant is also listed as an author) devotes an entire chapter to describing techniques and numbering them.

"It was just a way of teaching a technique and not having to talk through it every time, [so] ... if we said 6 technique, everybody on the staff and the squad knew what we were talking about," Gene Stallings wrote.

The "9 technique," for example, called for a defensive end to "take a short step with the inside foot toward the offensive end, and at the same time deliver a hand or forearm shiver to the head."

At practice, his coaches drilled the techniques into players with constant repetition. And Bryant, often from his lofty tower above the practice field, was alert to deviations.

Steve Meilinger, one of Bryant's stars at Kentucky, told Mike Bynum the following:

"Heck, Bryant could watch seven men do their stuff on offensive line play, and as though he had a photographic mind, he could tell each of the seven what he done wrong on a single play.

"He'd put an arm around an end and say: 'If you'd taken that step to the outside, then faked and come back in, you'd probably have had no problem with putting your block on the linebacker.' Then he'd make his point with the center, and on down the line.

"A man might not be born a football coach, but that kind of insight maybe has to be born in you."

"Coach Bryant changed football in the SEC in two pretty fundamental ways. One, he elevated the work ethic. He was the hardest working guy you've ever seen, and that meant the rest of us had to work harder coaching, scouting, recruiting, the whole bit. Two, his teams just played harder, and that meant our teams had to play harder to try to compete."

Vince Dooley

THE HATED SINGLE WING

Long after most teams had abandoned the single wing offense for the more explosive T formation, the University of Tennessee continued to run it. Bryant, who hated to lose to Tennessee, was always worried about the single wing. First, it was unfamiliar. Second, when the Vols ran their power sweep, it put tremendous pressure on the defensive ends.

At Kentucky, seeking to gain experience, Bryant scheduled North Dakota, another single wing team, the week before the Tennessee game. But North Dakota was no Tennessee. Kentucky led 70-0 at the half.

Bryant told his assistant Ermal Allen to take over and play Kentucky's scrubs in the second half. He took his first two teams—and maybe a few more—to an adjacent field and conducted a scrimmage.

> *"I'm no innovator. If anything, I'm a stealer or a borrower."*
>
> *Paul Bryant*

KEY ON THE GUARD

Darwin Holt tells this story to illustrate Bryant's knowledge of the technical side of the game.

Alabama was trailing Georgia Tech 15-0 at the half. Bryant told his team that they could still win, that the second half belonged to them.

Then he told Holt and Lee Roy Jordan, Alabama's linebackers, to watch Georgia Tech's guards, who were pulling to lead running plays. The 'backer across from the pulling guard was told to flow with the play; the other, to shoot the gap left by the guard.

Holt and Jordan spent most of the afternoon in the Tech backfield, and Alabama won, 16-15, on a last-second field goal by Richard O'Dell.

TACKLE ELIGIBLE

Coach Bryant loved the tackle-eligible play. When the split end on the tackle's side stepped back from the scrimmage line, becoming a split back, the flanker on the other side stepped forward, becoming an end. That made the tackle eligible to catch passes.

The play often worked. Its most successful practitioner was Jerry Duncan, who told Clyde Bolton how Alabama defended against the play when an opponent tried to use it against them. "The official would give his signal (indicating the tackle was eligible), and our defense would knock the tackle's butt off. There wasn't any way he was going to get out."

Ole Miss Coach John Vaught, burned twice by pass-eligible Alabama tackles, was a member of the college rules committee. According to David M. Nelson in his book, *Anatomy of a Game*, when no action had been taken on the rule as the 1968 meeting moved to a close, Vaught got up from the table, put a chair under the door knob, and said, "We are not leaving this meeting until we do something about that damn tackle-eligible pass."

The committee passed a rule requiring that five players with numbers between 50 and 57 be on the line of scrimmage, making the play illegal from then on.

THE 5' 7" END

Before the Alabama-Auburn game in 1959, Assistant Coach Jerry Claiborne noted that the Tiger defensive back in one-on-one coverage was vulnerable because of a tendency to come up too quickly.

Bryant and the other coaches devised a scheme to use Marlin Dyess, a 5' 7" halfback who weighed no more than 150 pounds, at split end. "If we get in this situation, we can score on it," Bryant said.

The Tide put in an "automatic" to take precedence over a called play if the right situation presented itself. In the third quarter, with Dyess in the game, quarterback Bobby Skelton zipped a pass into the flat. Dyess caught it, eluded the charging back, and ran for the only touchdown in the game. Alabama won 10-0. Auburn beat Alabama only once over the next ten years.

A COACH'S COACH

No college coach of his time commanded a bigger presence than Bear Bryant. He became an icon, a symbol of winning to players and coaches alike.

"He wasn't just a coach," former USC coach John McKay said. "He was the coach."

"Even his peers in the coaching business felt in awe of him," said Penn State's Joe Paterno. "He had such charisma. He was just a giant figure."

From former Nebraska coach Bob Devaney, "He was simply the best there ever was."

And finally, from the Bear himself, after the Tide beat Ohio State 35-6 in the 1978 Sugar Bowl: "Woody is a great coach, and I ain't bad."

ACADEMICS

EMPHASIS ON EDUCATION

Bryant insisted that his players get an education. Billy Neighbors, a freshman during Bryant's first year at Alabama, described getting a degree as "big to Coach Bryant." He tells the story of how the Coach invited him to lunch at a time when he wasn't doing well academically and was, in fact, cutting classes.

Neighbors realized the trouble he was in, but didn't think the coach knew. Imagine his surprise when he arrived at lunch to find that the dean was also joining them. Not only did the dean attend, he brought copies of Neighbors' academic record, including his IQ, and the documentation of how many classes he had missed.

Neighbors tried to avoid the coach by keeping his head down, but Coach Bryant said, "Look up at me, boy, I'm talking to you!" Bryant continued by addressing the dean, "Now this boy right here can help us win, but if he doesn't start getting better grades, he isn't going to be here!" Bryant further said, "I'm going to give him one more semester. I'm going to move him into my house with me, and I'm going to do him like I do Paul Jr. When he comes home with a C, I'll beat him with a damn dictionary."

Neighbors recalls that he "got straightened out real fast!"

LESSONS OFF THE FIELD

Bryant knew that there was more to a player than his abilities at football. The building of character was a strong component of Bryant's building of teams.

Players often talked about his emphasis on values to support their athletic abilities. Sylvester Croom noted that, "The biggest thing when you play for Coach Bryant are the lessons, the things he said over and over again."

Marty Lyons recalled, "I will always remember Coach Bryant saying, 'A winner in the game of life is that person who gives of himself so other people can grow.' ... I think the one thing Coach Bryant did was make you believe in yourself. He believed in his players, and by having him believe in you, it made you believe you could accomplish anything on and off the football field."

Academics

"Coach Bryant just made you a better football player than you thought you were. One of his philosophies was he could coach the average athlete and make him better and get 100 percent out of him. I think that is the true trademark of Paul Bryant."

Scooter Dyess

UNDER FIRE

THE HOLT-GRANING INCIDENT

The Bear's teams played hard, physical football. Bryant, especially early in his career, was contemptuous of teams that "wallow ... around all week playing 'drop the handkerchief.'" In his view, that was poor preparation for a game that involved whipping another team physically.

Among teams that were thought by some to be "wallowing around" was Georgia Tech. Coach Bobby Dodd had been highly successful in his approach, which, while it clearly wasn't "drop the handkerchief," relied less on hard, physical practices.

So it was the worst kind of bad luck and irony that it was in a game against Georgia Tech that an incident occurred that created the most painful episode in Bryant's career.

It happened late in 1961 in a game at Tech's Grant

Stadium, a game that Alabama was winning handily. Darwin Holt, one of Bryant's favorite players, was assigned to block for a punt return. As Tide halfback Billy Richardson ran up to field a shanked punt, Holt encountered Tech's Chick Graning running downfield to cover the punt.

At about the time the ball was fielded, Holt hit Graning with his forearm, which slipped under the single face-bar on the helmet, shattered the Tech player's jaw, and knocked out four teeth.

Once the extent of Graning's injuries was known, Atlanta newspapers went wild with recrimination, maintaining that the hit was not only illegal but that it also came after the whistle. (Films showed that it had not.) Holt, one writer said, had forfeited the right to play football. Others began to say that it was Bryant's doing because he taught "brutal football."

Bryant was defensive. He said he might have disciplined Holt himself if the Atlanta papers had not indulged in "crucifixion" of the Tide player. He pointed out to Atlanta writers that Tech, too, had been guilty of infractions. That only made the Tech supporters more angry.

Then *Atlanta Journal* sports editor Furman Bisher wrote an article for the *Saturday Evening Post* making the explicit charge that Alabama played "brutal football" under Bryant. Bisher wrote that "coaching intent" at Alabama was to knock opposing players senseless.

Bryant filed a libel suit against the *Post* that was still pending when the magazine dropped its other bombshell.

> *Turning down an offer to coach the Atlanta*
> *Falcons:*
> "Listen, there's not enough money in the U. S.
> Mint to get me into the same town with Furman
> Bisher."
>
> Paul Bryant

BEFORE THE JURY

In September 1962, a Georgia man somehow overheard a telephone conversation between Coach Bryant and former Georgia Coach Wally Butts. The man, George Burnett, took some notes. The notes made their way to officials at the University of Georgia and into the hands of the media. Eventually, the *Saturday Evening Post* ran an article stating that the conversation heard that day had been part of a "fix" of the Alabama-Georgia football game on September 22, a game won handily by Alabama.

Both Butts and Bryant sued the *Post* for libel.

Bryant testified at the trial of Butts' suit in Atlanta.

There was no mumbling. He was angry, and he showed it. He was, wrote author James Kirby in his book about the scandal, "the single most awesome figure this writer has ever seen in a courtroom, including lawyers and judges."

Alf Van Hoose, sports columnist for *The Birmingham News*, was at the trial and wrote the following about a moment when Bryant wanted to refer to some notes he had made about the game.

"He reached all over, chest pockets and side pockets looking for [his eyeglasses], and he had the jury, made up of middle-class Georgia people, on the fronts of their seats. Bryant kept searching himself. Then in a staged whisper he said, 'Damn, I left my eyeglasses on the plane.'

"At that moment, four jurors jumped to their feet, and one of them said, 'Here, Coach Bryant, try mine.'"

The attorneys at the publisher's table blanched.

Eventually, the jury found for Butts and awarded him over $3 million in damages. The amount was later reduced. Bryant and the *Post* settled out of court.

STANDING UP FOR PAT JAMES

Pat James played for Bryant at Kentucky and became one of his most active and enthusiastic assistant coaches. At Texas A&M, James said in the A-Club book of memories about the Bear, he [James] had been involved in a rules violation and thought he should resign.

"Patricia," Bryant told him. "If you leave, I'm leaving."

AGENT OF CHANGE

WHAT A FOOTBALL PLAYER LOOKS LIKE

For years, Bryant said that the social climate didn't allow him to go after black players. The story goes that this changed as a result of the 1970 USC-Alabama game at Legion Field in Birmingham. Bryant's Crimson Tide was made of all white players. When Trojan running back Sam Bam Cunningham and quarterback Jimmy Jones, both African-American, had good games, the University of Alabama was forced to realize that times were changing. An account of the game tells how Bryant took Cunningham to the Tide locker room and said, "This is Sam Cunningham. This is what a football player looks like."

*"In 1959 Coach Bryant brought his Alabama
team to Philadelphia to play Penn State in the
first Liberty Bowl. Not many leaders in the South
had the courage to leave the South and play an
opponent, much less one with a black player. He
always wanted Alabama to be more than a
regional team, and I think that is what separated
him from his peers in his conference and why
Alabama was a team with a national reputation."*

Joe Paterno

MAKING THE CHANGE

Alabama's spring practice in 1967 featured Dock
Rhone Jr., a guard from Carver High in Montgomery, the
first black football player ever to try out for the Crimson
Tide. Although he never played in a game, he marked the
beginning of the integration of the program.

Bryant recruited Wilbur Jackson in 1969 as Alabama's
first African-American scholarship player. The following
season, junior-college transfer John Mitchell became the
first black to play for Alabama. By 1973, one-third of the
team's starters were African-American.

*"From the first day as a freshman—and
freshmen were eligible for the varsity by then—I
could tell there'd be no such things as white
players and black players under Bear Bryant.
There'd just be football players."*

Sylvester Croom

HIS SPIRITUAL SIDE

HIS BELIEF

In his autobiography, Bryant said, "It has been important to me, my belief, if you want to call it that."

He frequently urged his players to attend church. He used biblical references to inspire them to better performance.

It's true that early in his career, he was profane in the extreme. And no one would contend that he followed Jesus's admonition to "turn the other cheek."

But his religious roots clearly influenced him in his later years.

Only a few days before his death, former quarterback Steadman Shealy, a minister, visited Bryant in his office, and the two prayed together. As Shealy was leaving, Bryant caught him by the arm and said, "You know, Steadman, in my own way, I bet I pray more than you do."

"If you want to be successful in life, you've got to get your priorities straight. Those priorities while you're in school should be: number one, your religion; number two, your family; number three, your education; then comes football."

Paul Bryant

TICKET TO HEAVEN

During a chance encounter with Dr. Robert Schuller, Coach Bryant expressed concern about whether he could actually claim to be a Christian. Dr. Schuller asked why he felt that way, to which the coach gave reasons that included, "Well, first off, Christians should have the feeling. And I don't." Also, "Then there's the part in the Bible where it says that these boys were teasing a prophet and the prophet called on God and God sent bears to eat the boys. I don't like that." Finally, he said, "And I know that if you're a Christian you don't do anything bad. You don't sin. Look at me. I'm smoking and drinking."

Schuller assured the coach that faith was more important than feelings, and that anyone who comes to God would not be cast out. Schuller continued by saying, "I can give you a ticket to Heaven right now." Schuller took the coach's boarding pass and wrote on it:

MY TICKET TO HEAVEN
"Anyone who comes to Me, I will not cast
out." Jesus Christ. Jesus said it. He is there. I trust
Him. I accept Him.

_____

Signature

Schuller challenged Bryant to sign it, and then he
reported that "an amazing thing happened. Bear Bryant
got a tear in his eye, and said, 'Oh, I like that. Can I keep
it?' I said, 'You bet. It's your ticket. I've got my own.'" He
folded it to fit his billfold, already thick with pictures and
important papers.

Schuller talked with the Bear again about this when
he asked his permission to share the story from the pulpit
in a service that would be broadcast on the popular *Hour
of Power* program. He thought the story might be too
personal to share, but Bryant said, "I'm proud of that, Dr.
Schuller. Don't edit it out. I still have that ticket. And I'd
be proud to have you tell that story to the whole country."
And so it was broadcast, just one day before Bryant died
of a heart attack.

"I don't know if I'll ever get tired of football. One time I thought I might. If I ever get that notion, I think back to one day I was out there on the practice field wondering about whether I'd get tired of the sport. Then I heard the Million Dollar Band playing over there on the parade grounds. When they started playing "Yea, Alabama," I got goose bumps all over me. I looked out there at those young rascals in those crimson jerseys, and I just wanted to thank God for giving me the opportunity to coach at my alma mater and be part of the University of Alabama tradition."

Paul Bryant

BABE PARILLI

Babe Parilli, an All-American starting quarterback for Bryant's Kentucky Wildcats, was, according to Bryant, "the best fake-and-throw-passer I have ever seen." But Parilli had badly injured his groin before the SEC opener against LSU and had been hospitalized with internal bleeding.

He got out of the hospital on the Friday before the game and never thought he would have to play in the game. But Bryant called him over before the pre-game warm-up and told him he wanted him in the game.

"Bigness is in the heart," he told Parilli.

Bryant put the Wildcats in a spread formation and dropped Parilli ten yards behind the center. Once he got the snap, he dropped back even farther.

"I think I could have played that game wearing a

tuxedo," Parilli said later. "I had such fantastic protection that nobody touched me all day."

Passing on almost every down, Parilli led Kentucky to two touchdowns in the first half. The Kentucky defense did the rest.

> *"Coach Bryant had the ability to make you feel like you were going to lose every game ... and he also had the ability to make you feel like you were going to win every game. That was the magic of his coaching ability, he could bring you to such a point that you were afraid that you were going to lose, but you also had a gut feeling that if you did what you were supposed to do ... what you were coached to do ... you could win, even if you were playing against better athletes."*
>
> *Jerre Brannen*

JOE NAMATH

A strange affinity—that might be an uninformed conclusion.

Joe Namath grew up in Beaver Falls, Pennsylvania, in a working class neighborhood of blacks, Poles, and Hungarians. He wore pegged pants and soft, Italian shoes, drove too fast, and hustled pool. He was brash and cocky.

Paul Bryant was from a backwoods family, stout in its fundamentalist Christian faith. He liked clean-cut kids who respected their elders.

Namath said that the first time they talked, atop Bryant's legendary tower, he understood nothing Bryant growled, except the word "stud."

But they had more in common than was immediately evident. They both loved betting on golf or backing a winning horse. They both loved to win. And they both loved the game of football.

Namath's path to Alabama and Bryant was a detour. He was headed toward Maryland but failed to qualify academically. No coach at Maryland wanted him to go to a rival, especially Penn State. One of them told Alabama's Charlie Bradshaw that Joe was available. Bryant sent Howard Schnellenberger to Beaver Falls to sign Joe and fend off other suitors.

Namath had a phenomenal gift for football. Bryant didn't say he was the best athlete he ever coached. He said he was the best he'd ever seen.

When Bryant suspended Namath in 1963 with Miami and the Sugar Bowl still to be played, he did it against the advice of all but one of his assistant coaches.

"Y'all aren't thinking of Joe," Bryant told them. "This is the best thing for Joe."

One person who was thinking about Joe was Mary Harmon Bryant. She sent for him secretly, and he spent several nights sequestered in the Bryant's basement. "When he got here, I hugged him and we both just cried like babies," she told a *Time* magazine reporter in 1980.

JOHN DAVID CROW

Bryant said that watching films of John David Crow playing high school football was like watching a grown man play against children.

But when Crow began practice at Texas A&M, Crow told Mike Bynum that he felt his hold on his starting halfback spot was tenuous.

"Coach Bryant had an uncanny ability to make me think my position was in jeopardy, even though all along he had me pegged as a starter," Crow said.

When Crow, who had built a successful real estate career, began to miss football, he went to see Bryant to ask him if he thought Crow should return to coaching.

Bryant spent two hours telling Crow what a lousy job coaching was and how crazy he would be to change careers.

A week or so later, Bryant called Crow and offered him a job as assistant coach at Alabama.

"Coach Bryant treats everybody the same, but he doesn't coach them the same."

Dude Hennessy

PAT TRAMMELL

Pat Trammell led the 1961 Alabama team to the National Championship, although, according to Bryant, he "had no ability as a quarterback."

But as a leader, he said, "I never had another like him."

Trammell was a big, tough kid from Scottsboro, Alabama, the son of a doctor.

According to Bill Oliver, Trammell, as a freshman, flipped a switchblade knife into the top of a table and asked the athletes there which ones were quarterbacks. No one was. "They all became halfback," Oliver said.

Most of Bryant's players were afraid of him and avoided direct conversation. Trammell, and a few others, craved the coach's company and would often stop in to talk with the Bear before practice. Trammell was a leader on the field, and he understood Bryant's system perfectly.

Despite the fact that he was a mediocre runner and passer, Trammell led the Alabama teams he played on to twenty-six wins, three losses, and four ties.

Trammell followed his father into medicine. When he

contracted cancer, Bryant twice traveled with him to New York to see specialists, but Trammell died at twenty-eight.

Bryant, who said Trammell was "the favorite person of my entire life," cried like a baby upon Trammell's death. It is no surprise, then, that upon hearing the news of his friend's passing, Bryant remarked, "This is the saddest day of my life."

BOB GAIN

Bob Gain and Paul Bryant didn't care much for each other.

Gain was a marvelous football player, still rated among the top one hundred of all time. He was big and fast, savvy and smart. In the days of early two-platoon football at Kentucky, he played both offense and defense.

But he felt that when he played under Bryant, the famous coach still had a lot to learn. He believed that Bryant cost Kentucky several games by overworking the Wildcats in practice.

Bryant, for his part, said in his autobiography that Gain "hated his guts."

Gain, as he grew older, developed a grudging respect for Bryant. Still, he denied ever writing him a letter that said "the things I hated you for then, I love you for now."

KEN STABLER

Maybe he had mellowed.

The way Ken Stabler remembered it, after he injured his knee early in spring training in 1967, his "give-a-shitter shorted out or something," and he started cutting classes and skipping practice.

Bryant sent him a telegram that said: "YOU HAVE BEEN INDEFINITELY SUSPENDED." Joe Namath then sent one that said, "HE MEANS IT."

Bryant let very few players who quit return to the team. He told Kenny, "You don't deserve to be on my football team." But after Stabler defied him and said he was "coming out [to fall practice] anyway," the Coach relented and allowed him to return.

Later, Bryant said in *Bear* that he might have made a mistake doing it. "I think it might have started us on that downslide, because for the next three or four years we weren't as tough or disciplined as we had been."

"I think the most incredible thing that they taught, to me, was here they were teaching twenty-year-old players who had been playing football since they were 8 or 10, how to put your hands down in a stance ... how to put your toes. How to make your first step, how to make your second step. The minutest detail for a lineman of every technique, it just fascinated me. It was a fascinating learning process, and I think that if I hadn't been committed to a medical career, I would have become a coach."

Butch Frank

LEE ROY JORDAN

Among all of Bryant's players, Lee Roy Jordan may have been the one who loved football the most.

His background was similar to Bryant's. He grew up on a cotton, corn, and peanut farm near Excel in Monroe County. His father, like Bryant's, was ill, and much of the work of running the farm fell on his mother. She was "the workingest human being in the world," Jordan told Richard Scott.

Jordan came to Alabama with the freshman class of 1959. He was small and wiry, the way Bear liked them in those days, and when he hit people, it "just sounded different," according to Tide assistant coach Clem Gryska.

Against Oklahoma in the 1963 Orange Bowl, Alabama's defensive scheme called on defensive linemen to take on blocks and allow the linebackers to fill the holes. Jordan made thirty-one tackles that day, in a game that Alabama won 17-0.

Jordan went on to an all-star career with the Dallas Cowboys, but he kept in touch with Bryant throughout his life.

OZZIE NEWSOME

When he first played football in the eighth grade, Ozzie Newsome told Richard Scott, "All I knew is when they threw it, I would catch it."

Newsome played in the early seventies, when Alabama was wedded to the wishbone offense. He knew he would catch more passes somewhere else, but he wanted to play for the Bear, "to play for the national championship behind the greatest coach."

In the run-oriented wishbone, Newsome caught 102 passes during his Alabama career, averaging more than twenty yards per reception, still the SEC record for a minimum of one hundred receptions.

One of Alabama's first black athletes, Newsome was named "Player of the Decade" by Alabama fans.

Newsome was once asked to compare the contributions of Coach Bryant and Martin Luther King Jr. "King preached opportunity," he said. "But without people like Coach Bryant who gave us the opportunity and really treated us as equals, where would we be?"

SOME WHO KNEW HIM

HOOTCHMAN

Merrill (Hootch) Collins was at Alabama when Bryant was a player and was still there when he returned as head coach. Hootch's job for many years had been to accompany the team on trips and look after the players' valuables during the game.

Later he aged in place, often sitting in a cane-bottom chair in the breezeway outside the athletic department door and kidding the players. Sometimes he would brew coffee for the coaches.

On many occasions after a brutal Bryant practice, Hootch would help exhausted players off the field and into the dressing room.

Hootchman was the only person anyone remembers who referred to Bryant as "boy." He told an interviewer that Bryant was just like any of the other players he had known in the old days at Alabama, "but more determined."

According to Pat James, Hootch once even had the temerity to bring a six-pack of beer into the coaches' dressing room. Coach Bryant was not amused. "Get it out of here," he said.

> *About coaching under Bryant:*
> *"He taught us to be winners on the field and throughout our lives."*
>
> Laurien Stapp

PAUL DIETZEL

Paul Dietzel, the highly successful coach at LSU, coached under Bryant at Kentucky. He recalled what happened after the Wildcats had been chewed up by the Tennessee single wing.

After the game, Bryant asked his coaches what had gone wrong. Dietzel said he offered the opinion that they had made a mistake in moving an inexperienced player, John Griggs, to defensive end.

"And boy, Coach Bryant really blew up," Dietzel said. "'Well, why in the blank-blank hell didn't you say that before?' I mean he really exploded.... He was just taking it out on me."

Dietzel said he got mad, too. "Well, coach if you didn't want my opinion, how come you asked me?" he said.

Not much more was said, but Bryant later gave Dietzel a plum scouting trip to New Orleans that Dietzel always felt was an atonement for the dressing room confrontation.

> *"He was a super guy to work for ... you just can't imagine how good he was to work for."*
> Phil Cutchin

JIM GOOSTREE

Goostree, the Alabama trainer when Bryant first came to the Capstone, was one of the few staff members who worked for J.B. "Ears" Whitworth who wasn't replaced.

On his first encounter with Goostree, the coach told him, "I know more about you than you know about me, and if you want to ... if you like me, and I like you, after spring practice, you've got a job at Alabama as long as you want one."

Goostree wanted one. After spring training, he told Bryant he was hoping to buy a new house and asked if he was going to be on the staff.

Bryant hardly looked up from his *Wall Street Journal*. "I sure as heck hope you will," he said. Goostree stayed on until Bryant's death in 1983.

> *"I don't hire anyone not brighter than I am. If they're not smarter than me, I don't need them."*
>
> Paul Bryant

HIS NEMESES

BOB NEYLAND

Bryant had a long friendship and deep admiration for the Tennessee's legendary Bob Neyland, known as "The General."

Bryant's Kentucky teams went 0-5-2 against Neyland. Neyland retired from coaching in 1952, and in 1953, Kentucky beat Tennessee 27-21.

The Bear's teams never beat Notre Dame, losing four games by a total of thirteen points.

And the Bear was just 1-7-1 against the University of Texas.

Of course, that meant the Bear was 322-69-14 against everyone else.

*"You never know what a football player is made
of until he plays against Alabama."*
"General" Bob Neyland

ADOLPH RUPP

Bryant found it hard to accept occasions when his
football program played second to Adolph Rupp's
basketball program at the University of Kentucky.

One particularly annoying incident was in 1950,
when the football team won its first Southeastern
Conference title. The basketball team also won the
conference title, hardly for the first time. After both teams'
seasons had ended, University boosters held a celebration
banquet, where they presented Rupp with a brand new
luxury automobile. Bryant, on the other hand, was given
a brand new Zippo cigarette lighter.

TEN BIG GAMES

1951 SUGAR BOWL:
KENTUCKY 13, OKLAHOMA 7

Kentucky was unbeaten through ten games in 1950, but lost its final game of the season to Tennessee, 7-0, in a game Bryant always believed he should have won. Kentucky was No. 7, the first time the Wildcats had ever finished in the top ten.

Oklahoma had won thirty-one in a row under Bud Wilkinson and was rated the nation's top team.

Bryant told John Underwood that he had a dream that led him to play what was essentially a 9-man line against the Sooners split-T.

In the first half, Vito "Babe" Parilli threw two touchdown passes and had another called back. In the third quarter, Oklahoma was at the Wildcats' goal line, but was turned back. They finally scored in the fourth quarter to make it 13-7, but the Kentucky offense then held the ball for the final seven minutes of the game in what Bryant said was "the loveliest non-scoring drive I ever saw."

1955: TEXAS A&M 20, RICE 12

In his second year at Texas A&M, Bryant had led his team to six wins with one loss and one tie and seemed assured of a seventh win against a mediocre Rice team. But nothing had gone right from the start, and when Rice scored two quick touchdowns in the fourth quarter, it looked bleak for the Aggies.

After the second touchdown, with a little less than three minutes left, Bryant told his team, "There is still time. You can still do it if you believe you can."

Bryant inserted a third-stringer, Loyd Taylor, at halfback. After an exchange of punts, Taylor circled end for fifty-five yards to the Rice 3, scored three plays later, and kicked the extra point to make it 12-7.

Jack Powell sent an onside kick spinning across the midfield line. Gene Stallings corralled it at the 43. Then quarterback Jimmy Wright rifled a pass that the apparently charmed Taylor caught near the goal line and scored. Another extra point made it 14-12. Rice fans were catatonic.

As were, evidently, the Rice players. Immediately, Jack Pardee intercepted a desperation pass, and A&M scored again to make the final 20-12. Writer Mickey Herskowitz, who missed the action on his trip from the press box to the dressing room, asked Bryant what had happened.

"Damned if I know," Bryant said. "I was too busy praying."

1956: Texas A&M 34, Texas 21

Was it a jinx? In thirty-two years, the Texas Aggies had never defeated the University of Texas at Memorial Stadium.

True, Texas A&M appeared to be far superior to the Texas team of 1956. The Longhorns had won just one game, against Tulane, in Coach Ed Price's final season. The Aggies were rated fifth in the nation, with only a tie against eight losses.

Still, a lot of Aggie teams had gone into Austin with high hopes that turned sour.

Coach Bryant didn't believe in jinxes. "You just go out and play the game, and if you're the best that day, you'll win."

Texas hung tough, fighting back twice from two-touchdown deficits to make it 20-14 at the half.

But the Aggies' Jack Pardee ran the second half kickoff back eighty-five yards, which led to an immediate touchdown. The final was 34-21.

The jinx, if there was one, soon reappeared. Coach Bryant left A&M for Alabama after the 1957 season. Texas A&M didn't beat Texas at Austin again until 1975.

1962 SUGAR BOWL:
ALABAMA 10, ARKANSAS 3

Bryant had told his first freshman class at Alabama—a group that included All-Americans Pat Trammell and Billy Neighbors—that if they followed his program, they could be national champions.

The prediction was actualized in the 1962 Sugar Bowl. But it wasn't easy.

Unbeaten Alabama took a 10-0 lead at halftime, on a twelve-yard run by Trammell and a Mike Davis field goal.

In the second half, the Alabama defense, which had allowed only twenty-two points all season, fought hard to keep the Razorbacks at bay. A field goal by Mickey Cissell made it 10-3. Arkansas' outstanding halfback Lance Alworth dropped what looked like a touchdown pass late in the game.

After the game, Bryant said, "Regardless of who was

coaching them, they would have been a great team. I said early in the season that they were the nicest, even the sissiest bunch I'd ever had. I think they read it, because later on they got unfriendly."

1965 ORANGE BOWL:
TEXAS 21, ALABAMA 17

Joe Namath re-injured his knee in practice just four days before the Orange Bowl game, played January 1, 1965. Unbeaten Alabama had been favored by six points. The line immediately fell back to even.

But Namath, in relief of Steve Sloan, who was also injured, came in and changed the game after the Tide fell behind 14-0.

Texas knew Namath was hurt, and the Longhorn strategy was to blitz. But Namath's release was quicker than his feet. He passed Alabama to a quick touchdown. Then Texas scored again to make it 21-7 at the half.

In the third quarter, Namath threw twenty yards to Ray Perkins for another TD. Another drive yielded a field goal, making it 21-17.

After Jimmy Fuller intercepted a pass, late in the game, Namath drove the Tide again to a first down at the 3. Three plunges by Steve Bowman got the ball inside the 1.

Then Namath himself, desperately plunging toward the goal line, was stopped "three fingers short." Bryant later said he had called the play—but it was Namath who actually did.

It was Namath's last game at Alabama. *The New York Times* said, "The 72,647 who filled the Orange Bowl Stadium were privileged to witness an exhibition that has hardly been surpassed in artistry, unruffled poise and deadly targetry."

1971: ALABAMA 17, SOUTHERN CAL 10

Bryant had his two worst years as an Alabama coach in 1969 and 1970, going 6-5 and 6-5-1. In the opening game of 1970, the Tide was embarrassed 42-21 when Sam Cunningham ran wild for Southern California.

Critics were asking if Bryant had lost his touch.

Bryant proved he had not. Three weeks before the season opener against USC, he made a bold move and secretly installed the wishbone offense, a triple-option offense that emphasizes the running game. The quarterback reads the defense and decides whether to give the ball to the fullback, a halfback, or to keep it.

Highly favored Southern Cal was completely surprised. Johnny Musso scored two touchdowns in the first half and a 17-0 lead that held up for a 17-10 win. The Tide won its next nine games and began a streak that carded fifty-three wins against only six losses through 1975.

> *"The Southern Cal game was the most exciting I ever played during my Alabama career."*
> Johnny Musso

1973 SUGAR BOWL: NOTRE DAME 24, ALABAMA 23

Coach Bryant was roundly criticized for this one. But the criticism was unjust.

The game was a classic confrontation between two outstanding college teams at the end of the 1973 season. (Usually played on New Year's Day, the Sugar Bowl this year was on December 31.) Alabama was unbeaten, and no opponent had come within fourteen points of the Tide. Notre Dame was also 10-0.

The game turned only at the end. The Irish led by one, beneficiaries of a ninety-three-yard touchdown run on a kickoff return. With only a few minutes left, Alabama stalled near midfield, and elected to punt. The punt was downed at the two-yard-line, but the Tide's punter was roughed by the Notre Dame charge.

Many assumed the Tide would be awarded an automatic first down, and television announcers said the same. But this was not the case. It was still fourth down. Bryant thought that there would be more ways to win with defense at the two-yard-line than with offense, fourth and five at midfield.

It almost worked. Notre Dame gained little on its first two tries. But on the third down, the Irish quarterback, Tom Clements, threw a play-action pass to tight end Robin Weber to escape the trap and cinch the game. The pass was so close to the sideline, Bryant said, he might have caught it himself.

1978: ALABAMA 38, MISSOURI 20

Alabama quickly took a 17-0 lead over Missouri in a game played in Columbia, Missouri, in 1978. Then the Tigers blitzed the Tide with three touchdowns in the second quarter and led at the half 20-17.

"It looked like they were going to run us out of the state," Bryant said.

To his players at halftime, Barry Smith recalled, he was scathing.

"You looked like a bunch of turds floating around out there," he told the players.

"And I want you to know I don't associate with people like that, and I'll not let a bunch of turds ride with me on that plane back home. I've got enough money in my pocket to buy every one of you a bus ticket back."

He told the defense they had four plays to stop the Tigers' next series, and the offense that they had one series to score. If they failed, he was going to use the third or fourth strings until someone stepped up.

On the first series in the second half, Missouri gained only five yards and tried to punt. E. J. Junior blocked it, and Ricky Gilliland ran it back thirty-five yards for a touchdown. Alabama won 38-20. Everyone rode back on the plane.

1979 SUGAR BOWL: ALABAMA 14, PENN STATE 7

Not much has ever matched the goal-line stand at the end of the 1979 Sugar Bowl.

Joe Paterno's Penn State Nittany Lions were unbeaten during the regular season. Alabama had lost once.

In the Sugar Bowl, the two teams played evenly for almost the entire first half. With 1:11 left on the clock in the first half, Alabama seemed likely to run out the clock.

Paterno, hoping to get the ball and a late field goal, called two consecutive time outs.

It backfired. Tony Nathan ran twice for thirty-seven yards, and then quarterback Jeff Rutledge found split end Bruce Bolton streaking through the end zone for a thirty-yard touchdown with only eight seconds left.

With just over four minutes left in the third quarter, Penn State tied the game after a pass interception set them up on the Alabama 48. But Alabama's Lou Ikner returned a punt sixty-two yards soon thereafter, and Major Ogilvie scored in the corner of the end zone three plays later.

Then came the goal-line stand that was immortalized by Daniel Moore's painting. The Nittany Lions recovered an Alabama fumble at the 19 and drove the ball almost to the goal line. The first try, from third and goal at the 1, failed to gain. An Alabama lineman growled at Penn State quarterback Matt Fusina, "You'd better pass."

On the next try, linebacker Barry Krauss and a tremendous Alabama line surge stopped Penn State tailback Mike Guman short. Bryant said, "That goal-line stand was something I'll never forget."

"Fourth down and a foot separating top-ranked Penn State from a possible national championship. Fusina hands to Guman—He didn't make it! He didn't make it! What an unbelievable goal-line stand by Alabama!"
            ABC Commentator Keith Jackson

315: Alabama 28, Auburn 17

Bryant entered the 1981 season with 306 wins, eight fewer than the all-time leader, Amos Alonzo Stagg.

At times during the season, it seemed unlikely that the Bear would pass Stagg before 1982. The team went 8-1-1 in its first six games.

Bryant's picture was on the cover of *Time*, but he was growing weary of the constant drumbeat of publicity. "This record business is old hat," he said. "I'll be glad when it's over."

Auburn had won five and lost five. But as everyone said, you could throw away the record book when it was the Iron Bowl.

And in fact, Auburn took advantage when Joey Jones fumbled two punts, and the team led 17-14 two minutes into the final quarter.

The lead didn't last. Tide quarterback Walter Lewis

found Jesse Bendross for a thirty-eight-yard touchdown. Linnie Patrick ran for another touchdown a few minutes later. The final was 28-17.

After the game, Bryant was proud to receive telephone calls from President Reagan and former President Jimmy Carter.

> *"Sure I'd like to beat Notre Dame, don't get me wrong. But nothing matters more than beating that cow college on the other side of the state."*
> *Paul Bryant*

SAYING GOODBYE

HANGING IT UP

With Alabama's unexpected losses in 1982, fans may not have been surprised when word leaked out on December 14 that Bryant would announce his retirement. But they were not, and never would be, prepared for the words that would conclude the career of their beloved coach.

There comes a time in every profession when you need to hang it up, and that has come for me as head football coach at the University of Alabama.

My main purpose as director of athletics and head football coach here has been to field the best possible team, to improve each player as a person, and to produce citizens who will be a credit to our modern day society.

We have been successful in most of those areas, but I feel the time is right for a change in our football leadership. We lost two big football games this season that we should have won. And we played in only four or five games like Bryant-coached teams should play. I've done a poor job coaching.

This is my school, my alma mater, and I love it. And I love the players, but in my opinion they deserve better coaching than they've been getting from me this year. My stepping down is an effort to see that they get better coaching from someone else.

It has been a great job for me, personally, to have the opportunity to coach at my alma mater. I know I will miss coaching, but the thing I will miss most is the association I have had with the players, the coaches, the competition—all those things that have made such a strong tradition at Alabama.

> *"His last year he was a very sick man, and he willed himself to live—that's exactly what he did. What was driving him to stay alive was to complete the season, to get things in order. I don't know if he himself knew how short his time was, but I think he had the drive and will to complete that season and to have things in order before he died."*
>
> Bryant Secretary Linda Knowles

FINAL GAME

Two weeks after announcing his retirement, Paul Bryant took his Crimson Tide to meet Illinois in the Liberty Bowl. The game, described as a thriller, ended with Alabama's 21-15 victory over their Big-10 rival. Although Bryant's post-game comments were always notable, his words following this, his last, were especially so.

I told the squad before the game that whether I liked it, whether they liked it, this would be a game all of us would remember the rest of our lives. I think it'll make my future years, or year, more pleasant. I'm thankful to have been associated with top-notch people throughout my career. I've been fortunate in that those people have reached most of the goals we've set throughout the years.

I'm tremendously proud of the team for winning. I'm flattered the team responded tonight like they did—I think they wanted it for themselves and for me.

I've looked at the last roundup forever, too, and this will make my memories a lot more pleasant.

THE END OF AN ERA

DEATH OF A LEGEND

He had been ill. But not many people knew it.

Bryant had been hospitalized for a while in the mid-sixties, suffered a heart attack in 1980, and then had a slight stroke in 1981. But he continued coaching, having often cracked that he would probably "croak in a week" if he were to quit.

When he did retire, he wrote all his former players, thanking them for their part in his career and urging them to "become even bigger winner[s] in life."

He was visiting his old business partner and fishing buddy, Jimmy Hinton, when his heart began its final revolt. He was rushed to Druid City Hospital, where tests revealed no major damage.

The next morning, he had visits from Sam Bailey, the associate athletic director, who had been with him for twenty-six years, and from his successor, Ray Perkins. Thought was being given to his release. There was laughter, joking.

But at 12:24 p.m. that afternoon, there was a sudden crisis. Bryant's breathing became labored, and his heart stopped beating. At sixty-nine, Bryant had suffered a coronary occlusion, the result of hardening of the arteries. Nothing the doctors and nurses did could help. He was pronounced dead at 1:30 p.m. on January 26, 1983.

The news stunned the state. Steadman Shealy, in a law class at Alabama, went out in the hall to bawl. John David Crow said he felt "numb." On radio talk shows, according to *Sports Illustrated*, callers "reached out for comfort, swapping accounts of personal encounters they'd had with the man, and openly crying on the air in a sort of down-home version of the Islamic mourners' public wailing."

Frank Broyles and Darrell Royal, playing golf, quit cold. Governor George Wallace ordered the state's flags flown at half-mast.

THE FUNERAL

Paul "Bear" Bryant's funeral was held in Tuscaloosa, Alabama, on January 28, 1983. Three churches were needed to contain the crowd that came to the service. Bryant's body was taken to Birmingham for burial at Elmwood Cemetery, in a caravan of three hundred cars. Three buses carried the entire 1982 team. Along the route, according to the Alabama highway patrol, as many as one hundred thousand people, many carrying handmade banners, waved the Bear goodbye. There were perhaps fifteen thousand people at the cemetery, quiet and respectful. The graveside ceremony was over quickly.

Remarkably, the death of Coach Bryant still stirs emotions long after the event. His former players at Maryland, Kentucky, and Texas A&M never forgot him. And for the people of Alabama, parodied and laughed at, derided as bumpkins and racists, he persists in memory like an Old Testament prophet who paved a path to excellence no one will ever match.

> *"Paul Bryant was a hard but loved taskmaster, patriotic to the core, devoted to his players, and inspired by a winning spirit that would not quit. Bear Bryant gave his country the gift of a life unsurpassed. In making the impossible seem easy, he lived what we strive to be."*
>
> *President Ronald Reagan*

JUST THE FACTS

PERSONALS

Born:	September 11, 1913
	Moro Bottom, Arkansas
Died:	January 26, 1983
	Tuscaloosa, Alabama
Mother:	Ida Kilgore Bryant
Father:	Monroe Bryant
Sisters/Brothers:	Barney, Orie, Harlie, Jack,
	Ouida, Kathryn, Louise, (Paul),
	Frances
High School:	Fordyce (Arkansas) High School
College:	Alabama
Wife:	Mary Harmon Black
	(June 2, 1935)

Children:	Paul Jr., Mae Martin
Height:	6'3"
Weight:	190 - 220

STATISTICS

Wins:	323
Losses:	85
Ties:	17

At Bryant Denny Stadium:
72-2-0 (57 consecutive wins between Oct. 26, 1963 and Nov. 13, 1982)

At Legion Field:
68-15-5

At Alabama Homecoming Games:
25-0-0

Against His Pupils (head coaches who either played for him or coached with him):

Charley McClendon	14-2
Bob Tyler	6-0

Bill Battle	6-1
Steve Sloan	5-0
Jerry Claiborne	4-0
Paul Dietzel	4-1
Charley Pell	1-0
Howard Schnellenberger	1-0
Larry Lacewell	1-0
Pat Dye	1-1
Gene Stallings	0-1
All	**43-6**

National Championships:
1961, 1964, 1965, 1973, 1978, 1979

SEC Championships:
Kentucky: 1950
Alabama: 1961, 1964, 1965, 1966, 1971, 1972, 1973, 1974, 1975, 1977, 1978, 1979, 1981

Coach of the Year:
National Coach of the Year: 1961, 1971, 1973

SEC Coach of the Year: 1950, 1961, 1964, 1965, 1971, 1973, 1974, 1977, 1979, 1981

Bryant as a Player and Assistant Coach:
384-100-25

Player

1933	Alabama	7	1	1
1934	Alabama	10	0	0
1935	Alabama	6	2	1
	Totals	**23**	**3**	**2**

Assistant Coach

1936	Alabama	8	0	1
1937	Alabama	9	1	0
1938	Alabama	7	1	1
1939	Alabama	5	3	1
1940	Vanderbilt	3	6	1
1941	Vanderbilt	6	1	2
	Totals	**38**	**12**	**6**

Head Coach

Maryland	6	2	1
Kentucky	60	23	5
Texas A&M	25	14	2
Alabama	232	46	9

Bryant's Winning Streaks

28 straight wins: last nine games of 1978 through seventh game of 1980

19 straight wins: entire 1961 season through eighth game of 1962

17 straight wins: final six games of 1965 through 1966 season and 1967 Sugar Bowl

Bryant's Bowl Record

1947	Great Lakes Bowl	Kentucky 24, Villanova 14
1950	Orange Bowl	Santa Clara 21, Kentucky 13
1951	Sugar Bowl	Kentucky 13, Oklahoma 7
1952	Cotton Bowl	Kentucky 28, TCU 7
1957	Gator Bowl	Tennessee 3, Texas A&M 0
1959	Liberty Bowl	Penn State 7, Alabama 0
1960	Bluebonnet Bowl	Alabama 3, Texas 3
1962	Sugar Bowl	Alabama 10, Arkansas 3
1963	Orange Bowl	Alabama 17, Oklahoma 0
1964	Sugar Bowl	Alabama 12, Mississippi 7
1965	Orange Bowl	Texas 21, Alabama 17
1966	Orange Bowl	Alabama 39, Nebraska 28
1967	Sugar Bowl	Alabama 34, Nebraska 7
1968	Cotton Bowl	Texas A&M 20, Alabama 16
1968	Gator Bowl	Missouri 35, Alabama 10
1969	Liberty Bowl	Colorado 47, Alabama 33
1970	Bluebonnet Bowl	Alabama 24, Oklahoma 24

1972	Orange Bowl	Nebraska 38, Alabama 6
1973	Cotton Bowl	Texas 17, Alabama 13
1973	Sugar Bowl	Notre Dame 24, Alabama 23
1975	Orange Bowl	Notre Dame 13, Alabama 11
1975	Sugar Bowl	Alabama 13, Penn State 6
1976	Liberty Bowl	Alabama 36, UCLA 6
1978	Sugar Bowl	Alabama 35, Ohio State 6
1979	Sugar Bowl	Alabama 14, Penn State 7
1980	Sugar Bowl	Alabama 24, Arkansas 9
1981	Cotton Bowl	Alabama 30, Baylor 2
1982	Cotton Bowl	Texas 14, Alabama 12
1982	Liberty Bowl	Alabama 21, Illinois 15

ARRIVALS AND DEPARTURES

1913
Born on September 11 in Moro Bottom, Arkansas.

1931
Left Arkansas in the rumble seat of Coach Hank Crisp's coupe.

1940
Left Alabama for assistant coach's job at Vanderbilt.

1942
Left Vanderbilt for the U.S. Navy.

1945
Left the Navy for head coaching job at Maryland.

1946
When Maryland President Curly Boyd reinstated a player Bryant had dismissed and fired an assistant coach without telling him, Bryant quit cold. Responding to a telegram, he took the head coaching job at Kentucky.

1954
Bryant had a love-hate relationship with Adolph Rupp, the legendary Kentucky basketball coach. In 1954, Rupp came under fire when three of his players admitted to shaving points for gamblers, and Bryant believed he would retire. When the announcement came that he had signed a new contract, the Bear quit and accepted the first job offered, at Texas A&M.

1957
Happy at Texas A&M where the military atmosphere fit his disciplinary ethic, Bryant was not anxious to leave. He had an opportunity to make millions in oil

through wealthy A&M alumni. But Alabama—which had tried to hire him before—appealed to his sense of family. "There's only one reason that I would consider [the Alabama job]," he told reporters. "When you were out playing as a kid, say you heard your mother call you. If you thought she just wanted you to do some chores, or come in for supper, you might not answer her. But if you thought she needed you, you'd be there in a hurry."

1958

"Mama" called, and Bryant left A&M for his alma mater. He returned to the Univeristy of Alabama and revitalized the Crimson Tide football program, turning it into the nation's top-ranked college team.

1982

Retired as head coach from the University of Alabama.

1983

Died suddenly in Tuscaloosa, Alabama, from heart disease.

IN HIS OWN WORDS

Coach Bryant is gone, but his values and achievements will live on in accounts of his life, and in the lives of those who remember him. As he often expressed, "The same things win today that have always won, and they will win years from now." Here are some of his memorable, and timeless, statements.

ON COACHING

"Mama wanted me to be a preacher. I told her coachin' and preachin' were a lot alike."

~

"The idea of molding men means a lot to me."

~

"The old lessons (work, self-discipline, sacrifice, teamwork, fighting to achieve) aren't being taught by many people other than football coaches these days. The football coach has a captive audience and can teach these lessons because the communication lines between himself and his players are more wide open than between kids and parents. We better teach these lessons or else the country's future population will be made up of a majority of crooks, drug addicts, or people on relief."

❧

"But it's still a coach's game. Make no mistake. You start at the top. If you don't have a good one at the top, you don't have a cut dog's chance. If you do, the rest falls into place. You have to have good assistants, and a lot of things, but first you have to have the chairman of the board."

❧

"Football changes and so do people. The successful coach is the one who sets the trend, not the one who follows it."

❧

"If there's one thing that has helped me as a coach, it's my ability to recognize winners, or good people who can become winners by paying the price."

❧

"Find your own picture, your own self in anything that goes bad. It's awfully easy to mouth off at your staff or chew out players, but if it's bad, and you're the head coach, you're responsible. If we have an intercepted pass, I threw it. I'm the head coach. If we get a punt blocked, I caused it. A bad practice, a bad game, it's up to the head coach to assume his responsibility."

❧

On Winning

"The price of victory is great, but so are the rewards."

❧

"If they don't have a winning attitude, I don't want them."

❧

"I don't want ordinary people. I want people who are willing to sacrifice and do without a lot of those things ordinary students get to do. That's what it takes to win."

❧

"If wanting to win is a fault, as some of my critics seem to insist, then I plead guilty. I like to win. I know no other way. It's in my blood."

❧

"My attitude has always been if it's worth playing, it's worth paying the price to win."

❧

"Winning isn't everything, but it sure beats anything that comes in second."

ON CHARACTER

"Show your class."

"Be humble. You don't have to tell anyone how good you are; just let your actions speak for you."

"I always want my players to show class, knock 'em down, pat on the back, and run back to the huddle."

"You don't measure a person's character by how hard he gets knocked down, but how well he gets up."

"You never know how a horse will pull until you hook him to a heavy load."

❧

"Set goals—high goals for you and your organization. When your organization has a goal to shoot for, you create teamwork, people working for a common good."

ON HARD WORK

"You may not always be as good as others, but you can always be better than yourself."

❧

"Don't do it the easy way, do it the right way."

❧

"I'm no miracle man. I guarantee nothing but hard work."

❧

*"It's not the will to win that matters—
everyone has that. It's the will to prepare to
win that matters."*

⁓

*"Little things make the difference. Everyone is
well-prepared in the big things, but only the
winners perfect the little things."*

⁓

*"There's a lot of blood, sweat, and guts
between dreams and success."*

⁓

*"Sacrifice. Work. Self-discipline. I teach these
things, and my boys don't forget them when
they leave."*

⁓

ON LOSING

Asked if any players were hurt in a losing game: "Every one of our boys had better have their feelings hurt. When you lose, something better hurt."

❧

After a loss to LSU: "When you get beat, no one can be satisfied, and around me they'd better not be satisfied."

After being asked if he had considered going for a field goal when trailing by three points: "Hell, no! A tie is like kissing your sister!"

❧

"It's awfully important to win with humility. It's also important to lose. I hate to lose worse than anyone, but if you never lose, you won't know how to act. If you lose with humility, then you can come back."

❧

"Losing doesn't make me want to quit. It makes me want to fight that much harder."

ON QUITTING

"The first time you quit, it's hard. The second time, it gets easier. The third time, you don't even have to think about it."

"Never quit. It is the easiest cop-out in the world. Set a goal and don't quit until you attain it. When you do attain it, set another goal, and don't quit until you reach it. Never quit."

"I'll never give up on a player regardless of his ability as long as he never gives up on himself. In time he will develop."

ACKNOWLEDGMENTS

There have been dozens of books about Paul "Bear" Bryant, and new biographies are still appearing. This book draws on the author's personal research and a wide range of published material. I have attempted in the text to acknowledge specific sources, and offer apologies to those I missed. In addition, I would like to thank the people at the Paul W. Bryant Museum for their assistance.

Books that were particularly useful were, of course, Bryant's 1974 autobiography, written with John Underwood, entitled *Bear*; *Coach Bryant's Football Family*, the A-Club Educational and Charitable Foundation's compilation of the recollections of many Bryant players, coaches, and acquaintances; Keith Dunnavant's *Coach*; Tom Stoddard's *Turnaround*; Kenny Stabler's *Snake*, written with Berry Stainback; Mark Kriegel's fascinating biography, *Namath*; and many others mentioned in the bibliography.

Vick Cross

BIBLIOGRAPHY

Bolton, Clyde. *They Wore Crimson*. Atlanta: Cromartie-Long, 1980.

Brooker, Tommy, ed. *Coach Bryant's Football Family: The Crimson Tide*. Tuscaloosa, AL: Alabama "A" Club Educational and Charitable Foundation, 1987.

Bryant, Paul, and Gene Stallings. *Bear Bryant on Winning Football*. Englewood Cliffs, NJ: Prentice-Hall, 1983.

Bryant, Paul, and John Underwood. *Bear*. New York: Little, Brown & Co., 1974.

Bynum, Mike. *Bryant. The Man, The Myth*. Atlanta, Cross Roads Books, 1979.

Bynum, Mike, and Jerry Brondfield. *We Believe: Bear Bryant's Boys Talk*. College Station, TX: We Believe Trust Fund, 1980.

Dunnavant, Keith. *Coach: The Life of Paul "Bear" Bryant*. New York: Simon & Schuster, 1996.

Forney, John. *Above the Noise of the Crowd. Thirty Years Behind the Alabama Microphone*. Huntsville, AL: Albright & Co., 1986.

Forney, John, and Steve Townsend. *Talk of the Tide*. Birmingham, AL: Crane Hill Publishers, 1993.

Herskowitz, Mickey. *The Legend of Bear Bryant*. New York: McGraw-Hill, 1987.

Nelson, Daniel M. *The Anatomy of a Game*. Cranbury, N.J.: Associated University Presses, 1994.

Norman, Geoffrey. *Alabama Showdown*. New York: Henry Holt & Co., Inc., 1986.

Kirby, James. *Fumble*. New York: Dell Publishing, 1986.

Kriegel, Mark. *Namath*. New York: Penguin Group (USA), 2004.

Peterson, James A., and Bill Cromartie. *Bear Bryant, Countdown to Glory*. West Point, New York: Leisure Press, 1983.

Bibliography

Scott, Richard. *Legends of Alabama Football.* Champaign, IL: Sports Publishing, 2004.

Stabler, Ken. *Snake.* New York: Doubleday, 1986.

Stoddard, Tom. *Turnaround. Paul "Bear" Bryant's First Season at Alabama.* Montgomery, AL: Black Belt Press, 2000.